The Hadith of
Malcolm X

aka El Hajj Malik Shabazz

The Hadith of
Malcolm X

aka El Hajj Malik Shabazz

by Brother James

A Publisher Trademark Title page

BBB
100 YEARS
Advancing Trust Together.

ASA Publishing Corporation
An Accredited Hybrid Publishing House with the BBB
(The Landmark Building)
23 E. Front St., Suite 103, Monroe, Michigan 48161
www.asapublishingcorporation.com

Copyrights©2017 Brother James, All Rights Reserved
Title: The Hadith of Malcolm X *aka El Hajj Malik Shabazz*
Date Published: 07.04.2017
Edition: 1 *Trade Paperback*
Book ID: ASAPCID2380689
ISBN: 978-1-946746-06-1
Library of Congress Cataloging-in-Publication Data

This book was published in the United States

A Publisher Trademark Copy page

Dedication

First, and foremost I dedicate this work to my Heavenly Father who is the sole source of my inspiration, my motivation and my dedication to be the best that I can be. It is through His divine guidance that I aspire to be an asset as opposed to a liability to the world community in general and the African and African American community to which I belong. Second, I dedicate this work to all the women of African descent, chiefly among them my Mother, who were an integral part of my intellectual, social and cultural development. Third, I dedicate this work to my earthly father and all my African American male mentors who taught me God's principles of having and maintaining a sense of propriety in all my dealings. Finally, I dedicate this book to my son Hamadi, who I pray to live long enough to see him have his on family.

Foreword

Many years ago while a student at the Ohio State University, I discovered a book entitled, "The Axioms of Kwame Nkrumah." This book, albeit succinct, had a profound impact on not only my life but my world view, morals, principles, and logic. I thought then, "what a wonderful tribute to a great leader to have his wisdom, predictions and philosophies presented in an easy to read and brief book." For years I toyed with the idea of putting such a book together on Malcolm X, whose writings also have had a profound impact on my life. Well, the days of toying with that idea are over. A literal definition for the word Hadith is, "the daily utterances of." The Prophet Mohammad was inspired by God to write the Holy Koran. In addition, he had a scribe who accompanied him everywhere and when he uttered his wise and prophetic sayings they were recorded in another book known as the, "Hadith." So herein lies my feeble attempt to capture the wisdom, philosophies, logic and prophesies of one of this world's most brilliant and articulate thinkers. It is with great pride that I offer this work to all those who admire Malcolm X and pray that its contents are of service to someone's scholarly pursuits.

2015 Foreword Addendum

Let us be ever mindful of the era, the epoch and the socio-economic and political environment that both produced and influenced Malcolm Little as he evolved or went through a metamorphosis into Malcolm X. The exact and same socio-economic and political environment that existed when Brother Malcolm X wrote these words, his worldview was the same environment that influenced the movement for equality and justice worldwide, led by men like Martin Luther King, Kwame Nkrumah in Ghana and Nelson Mandela in South Africa. The question that should be of tantamount importance for you the reader is, how much has changed in the capitalistic culture since the Prophet, Teacher, Minister and intellectual Malcom X passed? That is a question truly worthy of serious reflection, analyzation and concentration. Have the ways of the "world" changed for the better socially, economically, politically and more importantly, spiritually? What say you?

Table of Contents

Contents

Illustrations

General

The Hadith of

Malcolm X

aka El Hajj Malik Shabazz

The Hadith
of
El Hajj Malik Shabazz--aka
"Malcolm X:"

The Wisdom, Opinions, Philosophies,
and Prophecies of Malcolm X

1

A Brief Biographical Sketch of

Malcolm X (EL Hajj Malik Shabazz)

(1925-1965)

"Let all the enemies of the persecuted Blacks tremble ...

I am in earnest...

"I will not retreat a single inch...

and I will be heard!"

Malcolm X

Malcolm X was born Malcolm Little on May 19, 1925, in Omaha Nebraska to the Reverend Earl and Louise Little. Malcolm was the seventh son born to his father, a Baptist minister and organizer for Marcus Garvey's Universal Negro Improvement Association (UNIA). Malcolm's father consistently risked his life disseminating the philosophy of Marcus Garvey and the UNIA to the African American populations of Omaha and Lansing Michigan during the twenties. The philosophy of Garvey and the UNIA was that freedom, independence and self-respect could never be achieved by the African American, and therefore the African American should contribute to the rebuilding of Africa and leave the destiny of America in the hands of the Europeans who had conquered the indigenous populations and enslaved the African. It is a misnomer to subscribe to the notion that Marcus Garvey only advocated a "Back to Africa" movement. What Garvey did advocate was "Africa for Africans. A united Africa with Africans both on the native soil and those in the diaspora in control of the wealth derived from Africa. The Europeans had control of Europe why could the African not have complete and total control of Africa? Garvey and the UNIA were also advocates of racial purity, racial pride, and racial cohesion. Malcolm X was undoubtedly inspired and greatly influenced at an early age by his father's participation in the UNIA as an organizer. Malcolm's philosophies later in life were undoubtedly influenced by the ideas he heard his father and other UNIA members espouse while Malcolm attended UNIA meetings with his father as a young boy.

In 1931 when Malcolm was six years old his father was murdered in Lansing, Michigan for his role as an effective UNIA organizer. Malcolm X prophetically stated, "It has always been my belief that Ito (in addition to his father, five of Malcolm's uncle were to be murdered by white men) will die by violence. I have done all that I can to be prepared." After the death of his father, Malcolm's mother became ill and was unable to adequately care for her eight children. Malcolm and his sisters and brothers became wards of the state of Michigan. In 1940 at the age of fifteen, Malcolm went to live with his eldest sister Ella in Boston. While in Boston, Malcolm became well acquainted with the hustlers and criminal element of the predominately African American Roxbury section. The African American ghetto of Boston had a tremendous appeal and influence on the thought patterns and behavior of Malcolm because like many "Brain Washed" African Americans, he felt that he had to develop a Euro American image to achieve social status. Malcolm worked odd jobs in order that he might wear all; the fashionable attire and even went so far as to have his hair conked (processed to appear like the straight hair of Europeans). Of this act Malcolm was to later relate; "This was my first really big step toward self degradation: when I endured that pain, literally burning my flesh to have it look like a white man's hair. I had joined the multitude of Negro men and women in America who are brain washed into believing that Black people are "inferior' and white people "superior" - that they will even violate and mutilate their God created bodies to try to look pretty by white standards".

Malcolm became a leader of his peers in the streets of Boston. He was the premier street hustler and criminal and was viewed by his peers as a man who really knew how to beat the system. During World War II Malcolm moved to Harlem, New York and Detroit, Michigan where he applied his street expertise to acquiring large sums of money while doing little or no real work. Malcolm became very proficient as a thief, pimp, dope pusher and hustler to survive in the hectic and degrading fast paced world of the urban African American male. Malcolm was such a successful criminal that he was able to associate on a personal level with such notable African Americans as Billie Holiday and Redd Foxx. Malcolm had achieved the ultimate level of success in the urban ghetto or as he wisely put it; "In the ghettoes the white man has built for us, he had forced us not to aspire to greater things, but to view everyday living as survival and in that kind of community, survival is what is respected".

In 1946 at the age of twenty Malcolm Little was tried and convicted of burglary and sentenced to ten years in the Massachusetts State Prison at Charleston. While in prison, Malcolm Little's younger brother Reginald, came to visit him periodically and talked to him about the teachings of the Honorable Elijah Muhammad, the leader of a religious sect known as the "Black Muslims" and the "Nation of Islam". Malcolm was inspired and greatly influenced by the eloquent words of his brother Reginald who told him "You don't even know who you are. You don't even know, the white devil has hidden it from you, that you are of a race of people of ancient civilizations, and riches in gold and kings. You don't even know your true family name, you wouldn't recognize your true language if you heard it. You have been cut off by the devil white man from all true knowledge of your own kind. You have been a victim of the evil of the devil white man ever since he murdered and raped and stole you from your native land in the seeds of your forefathers. "Reginald told Malcolm that he should seek help from Mr. Muhammad, the faith leader of the Nation of Islam. Due to the influence of his brother,

Malcolm began to correspond with Mr. Muhammad.

The ensuing correspondence between Mr. Muhammad and Malcolm Little led to Malcolm acquiring an insatiable desire for the knowledge of African history. Prior to going to prison Malcolm had only acquired an eighth grade education. As Malcolm began to read more his level of consciousness began to rise correspondingly. The correspondence between Malcolm and Mr. Muhammad also led Malcolm to become more politically astute and develop "Black Nationalist" tendencies. Before being released from prison, after having served seven of the ten years he was sentenced to, Malcolm Little was converted to the Doctrines of the Nation of Islam. True Islam teaches that all men are brothers but the canons of Islam as practiced by the Nation of Islam dictate that: (1) that due to the oppression of Blacks by Europeans, all Europeans were devils and thus the natural enemies of Africans, and (2) that African Americans had to separate themselves from this devil race and be self-sufficient in terms of their socio-economic and political systems and needs.

After his release from prison in 1953, Malcolm X became a minister and organizer for the Nation of Islam. It was Malcolm's specific duties to travel across the country on speaking tours and establish Black Muslim Mosques in any and all cities where African Americans were receptive to the Black Nationalist views espoused by the Nation of Islam. Almost immediately Malcolm noticed that as a recruiter - organizer for the Nation of Islam, that his most valuable asset was his "Street Smarts". Malcolm was able to communicate easily with the grass roots African Americans because he had once been among their numbers.

Malcolm was also aware of the plight of African American people economically incarcerated in the ghettoes of urban America because he was once incarcerated in the socio-economic prisons of Detroit, Harlem, and Boston. It was due to this quality of communication and level of understanding that Malcolm was successful in converting those people this society views as unredeemable and social outcast. Malcolm was able to convert the dope addicts, pimps, prostitutes and drug pushers. He was also able to convert to the Nation of Islam, African Americans who were former Christians but felt the need for a religiously ideological Black Nationalist oriented movement. The scope of which would be to bring an abrupt end to those policies which tended to adversely affect them.

Malcolm was instrumental in the formation of the Nation of Islam's newspaper, Muhammad Speaks and the formation of numerous Mosques across the country. During the later 1950s and the early 1960s Malcolm was in great demand to speak on college campuses and to be interviewed on radio and television. People, African and Euro Americans alike began to look to Malcolm X as the true (defacto) leader of the Nation of Islam instead of Elijah Muhammad. Malcolm's popularity in the African American community threatened the leadership position of the Honorable Elijah Muhammad. This perceived decline in power led Mr. Muhammad to attack Malcolm as someone who lived to be in front of the cameras and microphones of the media. Malcolm was also criticized by

Mr. Muhammad for his espousal of a "Black" separatist ideology; Pan Africanism, and the lack of non-religious political action by the Nation of Islam. The relationship between these men was further strained by allegations that Mr. Muhammad had fathered several illegitimate children by some of the Nation of Islam faithful. In 1964 Mr. Muhammad, feeling threatened by Malcolm's rising popularity had him silenced as the National Spokesperson for the Nation of Islam. Mr. Muhammad's rationale was Malcolm's comment that the assassination of John F. Kennedy was an example of "chickens coming home to roost" (what Malcolm was obviously referring to was that America was a violent society, where little had been done to curtail this violence thereby making it easy for the highest official in the land to be a victim of violence). Malcolm, realized he had done his job TOO well and was slowly being phased out of the national limelight of the Nation of Islam. Malcolm once stated, "I had enough experience to know that in order to be a good organizer of anything which YOU expect to succeed - including yourself - you must almost mathematically analyze cold facts". It is ironic that Malcolm's dedication and persistence ultimately led to his being expelled as a minister and organizer, jobs he had excelled in, for the Nation of Islam.

After his split with the Nation of Islam in March 1964 Malcolm began to address two major areas of concern which he felt were the Nation of Islam's shortcomings. These two areas of concern were: (1) the lack of a Black Separatist ideology, and (2) the non-religious political action of the Black Muslims. Malcolm's solution to the problem of the lack of a

Black Nationalist ideology was to promote Pan Africanism. The theory of Pan Africanism succinctly put, is the total unification for the total liberation of people of African descent no matter where they were located around the world.

In 1964 Malcolm traveled to the Holy city of Mecca (in Saudi Arabia) to fulfill a religious obligation for all orthodox Muslims known as the Hajj. The Arabic interpretation of hajj is to set out toward a specific goal. In Islamic law it means to set out for Ka'ba (Sacred House) and fulfill the pilgrimage rites. The Holy Koran states, "Pilgrimage to the Ka'ba is a duty men owe to God; those who are able, make the journey". While in Mecca Malcolm was awestruck by the massive crowds of pilgrims of every race and color who made no distinction based upon race, color or national origin. Witnessing this peaceful coalescence was to have a profound effect on Malcolm. At this point he began to reevaluate what he had been taught by Mr. Muhammad, that all Europeans were evil and devils. Malcolm still believed however, that African Americans should maintain separate organizations to achieve their goals of human and civil rights.

In 1964 Malcolm also traveled extensively in Africa talking to such noted African leaders and proponents of Pan Africanism as Kwame Nkrumah, President of Ghana, and Sekou Toure, President of Guinea. Malcolm's solution to the non-religious political action was the formation of the Organization of Afro-American Unity (OAAU). Malcolm saw the need for an umbrella Black Nationalist organization that could financially, spiritually, and physically aid African Americans struggling for civil rights. Malcolm felt that the

OAAU should send some of its members to those southern states where African Americans demonstrating for their civil rights were victims of violent and racist attacks by Euro Americans to protect these African Americans from these violent and racist attacks.

Malcolm's advocacy of a militant and unified Black Nationalist organization at a time when the majority of African Americans were voluntarily and peacefully participating in "Peaceful" demonstrations where brute force was used against them, threatened the power structure of this country. Basically, Malcolm and the OAAU advocated that:

- African Americans could only get their true freedom by fighting for it even if that led to Bloodshed;

- that the U. S. government was a racist government and had no intention of granting total equality to African Americans;

- that gradualism, the program of the liberals was not the true road to equality;

- That "Uncle Toms" or "race traitors" must be exposed and opposed;

- that African Americans must rely on themselves and control their own struggle;

- that African Americans must determine their own strategy and tactics and;

• African Americans must select their own leaders

Because of the views Malcolm espoused and his tremendous gift as an orator and organizer, he was perceived as a major threat to the American way of life. Malcolm X was assassinated on February 21, 1965, while delivering an address at the Audubon auditorium in New York City. His wife and children were in attendance and witnessed his assassination. Even though the three assassins were tried, convicted and imprisoned for killing Malcolm the person or person who instigated them remains unknown. The media suggested that the assassins were agents of the Nation of Islam; however, there is a great deal of evidence that suggests that federal agents working for the FBI and CIA may have played a significant role.

Malcolm X employed political education as the basis of his plans to uplift the material conditions of African American people. Malcolm analyzed and then realized that in order to alleviate the problems created by the environing group in this country, particularly racism that African Americans needed to understand their cultural heritage; seek the positive elements from traditional African society and apply these positive traits and customs to their conditions the world over. This could only be done by revolutionary thoughts and revolutionary deeds. Malcolm advocated that African Americans should no longer strive to emulate and assimilate into the cultural value systems of the Euro-Christian west. This advocacy was based upon the realization that the cultural and value systems imposed on African Americans by the environing group was totally unsatisfactory. In order to be accepted in this society, African Americans had to try to look like, talk like, and live like members of the environing group, while simultaneously divorcing themselves from any and all traits or natural characteristics which were not Euro-Christian in origin. Malcolm saw that oppression and racism even extended itself into the realm of identity. By this I suggest that as African Americans we are somewhat hesitant to proudly say "I am an African American" with the same fervor as an Italian American, German American or Irish American would boast of their national origin. African Americans, Malcolm perceived, were given a classification by the Euro-Christian which denied them a national identity and a land base. This classification was the term "Negro" which only implies a color - black, and creates a subservient mentality.

To alleviate the adverse psychological effects associated with the slave mentality and the acceptance of the classification of "Negro", Malcolm spoke on numerous college campuses, in African American churches and used whatever forum was available to espouse the importance of studying African History. His knowledge of African History led Malcolm to be viewed by the African American masses as a charismatic leader. Malcolm used his charisma and his intellect to promote Pan Africanism at a level that was readily understood by the masses of his people and the African American intelligentsia. Malcolm believed that once African Americans realized what produced their problems then they only needed to attain and maintain a consistent ideological goal which would eventually eliminate their problems "By any means necessary".

It may be concluded that Malcolm X was instrumental in identifying the source of the problems African Americans faced; made African Americans aware of the political and socio-economic contradictions or cultural distortions within this country; organized the masses in an attempt to destroy racism, and build a more equitable socio-economic system. African Americans looked to Malcolm for political and historical education, ideological clarity and increased race consciousness. Malcolm's prophetic teachings and political astuteness, his brilliant articulate grass roots orations, and his mass appeal clearly indicate that he was a visionary whose spirit still guides the people of conscience today.

Malcolm X on:

-Identity-

We don't think as Americans any more, but as a Black man. With the mind of a Black man, we look beyond America. And we look beyond the interest of the white man.

Malcolm X: The Last Speeches, page 45

There are more Africans in Harlem than exist in any city on the African continent. Because that's what you and I are, Africans.

Malcolm X: By Any Means Necessary (OAAU Founding Rally), page 39

The Black man's history - when you refer to him as the Black man you go way back, but when you refer to him as a Negro, you can only go as far back as the Negro goes. And when you go beyond the shores of America you can't find a Negro. So if you go beyond the shores of America in history, looking for the history of the Black man, and you're looking for him under the term Negro, you won't find him. He doesn't exist. So you end up thinking that you didn't play any role in history.

Malcolm X on Afro-American History, page 18 - 19

When I say Africans aboard and Africans here in this country - the man you call the Negro is nothing but an African himself. Why, some of them have been brainwashed into thinking that Africa is a place with no culture, no history, no contribution to civilization or society.

Malcolm X: The Last Speeches, page 26

The African get respect because he has an identity and cultural roots. But most of all because the African owns some land. For these reasons he has his human rights recognized, and that makes his civil rights automatic.

Malcolm X: As They Knew Him, page 126

To the same degree Africa is independent and respected we are independent and respected, but to the degree we are disrespected the Africans are also disrespected. Our origin is the same and our destiny is the same, whether we like it or not.

Malcolm X: By Any Means Necessary, page 122

Africa will not go forward any faster than we will and we will not go forward any faster than Africa will. We have one destiny and we've had one past.

Malcolm X: By Any Means Necessary, page 40

-The Study of History-

Of all our studies, history is best qualified to reward our research. When you see you have problems ... examine the historic method used all over the world by others who have problems similar to yours. Once you see how they got theirs straight, then you know how to get yours straight.

Malcolm X Speak, page 8

Only the poor, brainwashed American Negro has been made to believe that Christ was white, to maneuver him into worshiping the white man. After becoming a Muslim in prison, I read almost everything I could put my hands on in the prison library. I began to think back on everything I had read and especially with the histories, I realized that nearly all of them read by the general public have been made into white histories. I found out that the history- whitening process either had left out great things that black men had done, or some of the great black men had been whitened.

Malcolm X As They Knew Him, page 119

History is the long and tragic story of the fact that privileged groups seldom give up their privileges voluntarily.

History is a people's memory and without memory, man is demoted to the level of the lower animals.

My Soul Looks Back, Less I Forget, page 190

He [the African Americans of his day] knows nothing about the ancient Egyptian civilization on the African continent. Or the ancient Carthaginian civilization on the African continent. Or the ancient civilizations of Mali on the African continent. Civilizations that were highly developed and produced scientists. Timbuktu, the center of the Mali Empire, was the center of learning at a time when the people up in Europe didn't even know what a book was. He doesn't know this, because he hasn't been taught.

Malcolm X: The Last Speeches, page 37-38

I say sir, that you can never make an intelligent judgement without evidence. If any man will study the entire history of the relationship between the white man and the Black man, no evidence will be found that justifies any confidence or faith that the Black man might have in the white man today.

Malcolm X: As They Knew Him, page 118

Whole Black empires, like the Moorish, have been whitened to hide the fact that a great Black empire had conquered a white empire even before America was discovered. The Moorish civilization - Black Africans - conquered and ruled Spain; they kept the light burning in Southern Europe.

Malcolm X: As They Knew Him, page 119

-Capitalism-

After four hundred years of slave labor, we have some back pay coming. A bill that is owed to us and must be collected. If the government of America truly repents of its sins against our people and atones by giving us our true share of the land and the wealth, then America can save herself. But if America waits for God to step in and force her to make a just settlement, God will take this entire continent away from the White man. And the Bible says that God can give the kingdom to whomever he pleases.

Malcolm X: The End of White World Supremacy
(The Black Revolution), page 75

Better jobs won't solve our problems. An integrated cup of coffee isn't sufficient to pay for four hundred years of slave labor.

Malcolm X: The End of White World Supremacy
(The Black Revolution), page 73

Our people in the Negro community are trapped in a vicious cycle of ignorance, poverty, disease, sickness, and death. There seems to be no way out. No escape.

Malcolm X: The Last Speeches, *page 64*

You show me a capitalist; I'll show you a bloodsucker.

"Malcolm X Speaks" (At the Audubon), *page 121*

Unemployment and poverty have forced many of our people into this life of crime; but ... the real criminal is in city hall downtown. The real criminal is in the State House in Albany. The real criminal is in the White House in Washington, D. C. The real criminal is the white man who poses as a liberal- the political hypocrite. And it is these legal crooks, posing as our friends, [who are] forcing us into a life of crime and then using us to spread the white man's evil vices among our own people. Our people are scientifically maneuvered by the white man into a life of poverty. You are not poor accidently.

He maneuvers you into poverty. You are not a drug addict accidently. Why, the white man maneuvers you into drug addiction. You are not a prostitute accidently. You have been maneuvered into prostitution by the American white man. There is nothing about your condition here in America that is an accident.

Martin & Malcolm & America, *page 89*

What is looked upon as an American dream for white people has long been an American nightmare for black people.

Martin & Malcolm & America, page 89

People are always speculating - why am I as I am? To understand that of any person, his whole life, from birth, must be reviewed. All our experiences fuse into our personality.

Everything that ever happened to us is an ingredient.... I think that an objective reader may see how in the society to which I was exposed as a black youth here in America, for me to wind up in prison was really about inevitable.

The Autobiography of Malcolm X

They promised us jobs and gave us welfare checks instead; we're still jobless; still unemployed; the welfare is taking care of us, making us beggars, robbing us of our dignity, our manhood.

Malcolm X Speaks (Prospects of Freedom in 1965J), page 155

If God's unchanging laws of justice caught up with every one of the salve empires of the past, how dare you think White America can escape the harvest of unjust seeds by her white forefathers against our Black forefathers here in this land of slavery

Martin & Malcolm &America, *page 159*

If you can't receive justice in a man's house that man deprives you of justice, he should let you leave. And if he doesn't want you to leave his house, yet he can't give you justice in the house, he'll end up losing the whole house himself. This is what America is faced with.

Malcolm X: The Last Speeches, *page 53*

-Participation in the Democratic Process-

No I'm not an American. I'm one of the 22 million black people who are victims of Americanism. One of the... victims of democracy, nothing but disguised hypocrisy. So I'm not standing here speaking to you as an American, or a patriot, or a flag saluter, or a flag waver - no, not I! I'm speaking as a victim of this American system. And I see America through the eyes of the victim. I don't see any American dream; I see an American nightmare.

Malcolm x Speaks (The Ballot or the Bullet), *page 26*

You don't catch hell because you're a Baptist, and you don't catch hell because you're a Methodist.... You don't catch hell because you're a Democrat or a Republican, you don't catch because you're a Mason or an Elk, and you sure don't catch hell because you're an American; because if you were an American, you wouldn't catch hell. You catch hell because you're ... Black.... You catch hell; all of us catch hell for the same reason.

Martin & Malcolm & America, *page 115*

Imagine that - a country that's supposed to be a democracy, supposed to be for freedom and all that kind of stuff when they want to draft you and put you in the army and send you to Saigon to fight for them - and then you've got to turn around and all night long discuss how you're going to just get a right to register and vote without getting murdered. Why, that's the most hypocritical government since the world began.

Martin & Malcolm & America, *page 115*

Well independence only comes by two ways; by the ballots or by bullets. What you read historically - historically you'll find that everyone who gets freedom, they get it through ballots or bullets. Now naturally everyone prefers ballots, and I even prefer ballots but I don't discount bullets. I'm not interested in either ballots or bullets, I'm interested in freedom!

Malcolm X: As They Knew Him, *page 170*

We propose to support and organize political clubs, to run independent candidates for office and to support any Afro-American already in office who answers to and is responsible to the Afro-American community. We don't support any Black man who is controlled by the white power structure.

Malcolm X: By Any Means Necessary, *page 46*

-Being a Muslim-

The people in the Muslim world don't regard a man according to the color of his skin. When you are a Muslim you don't look at the color of a man's skin whether he is black, red, white, or green or something like that; when you are a Muslim you look at the man and judge him according to his conscious behavior.

Malcolm X: The FBI File£, *page 237*

In other words a Muslim is one who strives to live a life of righteousness.

Malcolm X: The End of White World Supremacy, *page 69*

True Islam removes racism, because people of all colors and races who accept its religious principles and bow down to the one God, Allah, also automatically accept each other as brothers and sisters, regardless of differences in complexion.

Malcolm X Speaks (Letters from Abroad), page 60

It could be heard increasingly in the Negro communities "Those Muslims talk tough, but they never do anything unless somebody bothers Muslims." I moved around among outsiders more than most other Muslim officials. I felt the very real potentially that, considering the mercurial moods of the Black masses) this labeling of Muslims as "talk only" could see us, powerful as we were) one day suddenly separated from the Negroes' front-line struggle.

Malcolm X: The FBI File, page 34

You can go to any small Muslim child and ask him where hell is or who is the devil and he wouldn't tell you that hell is down in the ground or that the devil is something invisible that you can't see. He'll tell you hell is right where he has been catching it and he'll tell you the one who is responsible for him having received this hell is the devil.

Malcolm X: The FBI Files, page 164

We believe that when God comes to establish the religion of Islam or the kingdom of Islam or the world of Islam, he can't do so without first destroying all other religions, governments, nations, and worlds that stand in his way.

Malcolm X: The Last Speeches, *page 75*

....I have had a chance to do some traveling and travel broadens ones scope, and as a Muslim whose religion is Islam, as it is practiced and taught in the Muslim world, I realize that it is impossible to call oneself a Muslim, to call one's religion Islam and at the same time judge a man by the color of his skin.

Malcolm X: The FBI File, *page 345*

-Hate-

As soon as the white man hears a Black man say he's through loving white people, then the white man accuses the Black man of hating him.

Malcolm X: As They Knew Him, *page 114*

Wherever we look today, whether it be in the South, the North, the East, or the West, we see ever increasing racial tensions.

Malcolm X: The Last Speeches, *page 60*

When a high-powered rifle slug tore through the back of NAACP Field Secretary Medgar Evers in Mississippi, wanted to say the blunt truths that need to be said. When a bomb was exploded in a Negro Christian church in Birmingham, Alabama, snuffing out the lives of those four beautiful little Black girls, I made comments -- but not what should have been said about the climate of hate that the American white man was generating and nourishing.

Malcolm X: The FBI File, page 35

How can anybody ask us do we hate the man who kidnaped us four hundred years ago, brought us here and striped us of our history, stripped us of our culture, stripped us of our language, stripped us of everything that you could use today to prove that you were part of the human family, brought you down to the level of an animal, sold you from plantation to plantation like a sack of wheat, sold you like a sack of potatoes, sold you like a horse and a cow, and then hung you up from one end of the country to the other, and then you ask me do I hate him? Why, your question is worthless!

Malcolm X: The End of White World Supremacy
(The Black Revolution), page 79

We have been a people who hated our African characteristics. We hated our heads, we hated the shape of our nose, we wanted one of those long dog like noses ...we hated the color of our skin, hated the blood of Africa that was in our veins; we had to end up hating ourselves.

Malcolm X Speaks (After The Bombing), *page 169*

The colonial powers of Europe ... always project Africa in a negative light: jungle savages, cannibals, nothing civilized ... It was negative to you and me, and I began to hate it ... In hating Africa and in hating the Africans, we ended up hating ourselves without ever realizing it.

We're anti-evil, anti oppression, anti-lynching. You can't be anti those things unless you're also anti-the oppressor and the lyncher. You can't be anti-slavery and pro-slave master; you can't be anti-crime and pro-criminal.

Martin & Malcolm & America, *page 101*

You hear us talking about the white man and you want to go away and tell him we have been subversive. Here is a man who raped your mother and hung your father on his tree, is he subversive? Here is a man who robbed you of all knowledge of your nation and you religion and is he subversive? Here is a man who lied to you and tricked you about all things, is he subversive?

Martin & Malcolm &America, *page 94*

I know that you don't realize the enormity, the horrors, of the so-called Christian white man's crime.... Not even in the Bible is there such a crime! God in his wrath struck down with fire perpetrators of lessor crimes! One hundred million of us Black people! Your grandparents! Mine! Murdered by this white man. To get fifteen million of us here to make us slaves, on the way he murdered one hundred million! I wish it was possible for me to show you the sea bottom in those days - the Black bodies, the blood, the bones broken by boots and clubs!

The pregnant Black women who were thrown overboard if they got sick! Thrown overboard to the sharks that learned that following these ships was the way to grow fat! Why, the white man's raping of the Black race's woman began right on those slave ships! The blue eyed devil could not even wait until he got them here! Why, brothers and sisters, civilized mankind has never known such an orgy of greed and lust and murder...

Martin & Malcolm & America, page 97

If it is not hate to say how the white man stole this country from the Indians, then why is it hate to teach our people how this same white man kidnaped us from the East, brought us here in chains, stripped us of our ancient culture, robbed us of all knowledge concerning our glorious history and then made us slaves?

Martin & Malcolm & America, page 177

-Civil and Human Rights-

The whites don't have to go to the Supreme Court or before the President for freedom. don't see where Black people should have to wait for some presidential proclamation or some senator or congressman to make up his mind that we are free.

Malcolm X: The FBI Files, page 241

I believe in the brotherhood of man. But despite the fact that I believe in the brotherhood of man, I have to be a realist and realize that here in America we're in a society that doesn't practice brotherhood. It doesn't practice what it preaches. I preach brotherhood, but it doesn't practice brotherhood.

Malcolm X: The Last Speeches, page 157

Hell is when you're dumb. Hell is when you're a slave. Hell is when you don't have freedom and when you don't have justice. And when you don't have equality, that's hell.... And the devil is the one who deprives you of justice.... equality... civil rights. The devil is the one robs you of your right to be a human being. I don't have to tell you who the devil is.

Martin & Malcolm & America, page 174

I'm for truth, no matter who tells it. I'm for justice, no matter who it is for or against. I'm a human being first and foremost, and as such I'm for whoever and whatever benefits humanity as a whole.

Martin & Malcolm & America, page 181

Sometimes, I have dared to dream ... that one day, history may even say that my voice - which disturbs the white man's smugness, and his arrogance, and his complacency - that my voice helped to save America from a grave, possibly even final catastrophe.

Martin & Malcolm & America, page 181

You don't have to be a man to fight for freedom. All you have to do is to be an intelligent human being.

Martin & Malcolm & America, page 212

The price of freedom is death.

Martin & Malcolm & America, page 288

Respect me or put me to death.

Martin & Malcolm & America, page 288

It is time for martyrs now, and if I am to be one, it will be for the cause of brotherhood. That' is the only thing that can save this country.

Martin & Malcolm & America, *page 315*

Actually you cannot separate peace from freedom because no one can be at peace unless he has his freedom.

Malcolm X Speaks (Prospects for Freedom in 19651, *page 148*

It's not wrong to expect justice. It's not wrong to expect freedom. It's not wrong to expect equality. If Patrick Henry and all of the Founding Fathers of this country were willing to lay down their lives to get what you are enjoying today, then it's time for you to realize that a large, ever increasing number of Black people in this country are willing to die for what we know is due us by birth.

Malcolm: The Last Speeches, *pages 55-56*

-Land (Ownership)-

Land is the basis of all economic security. Land is essential to freedom, justice, and equality. Land is essential to true independence.

Malcolm X: The last Speeches, page 69

-Integration-

Integration in America is hypocrisy in the rawest form. And the whole world can see it.

Malcolm X: The Last Speeches, page 43

We are not fighting for integration, nor or we fighting for separation. We are fighting for recognition as human beings.

Martin & Malcolm & America, page 181

I don't see how you could call rapid strides being made in the field of integration where you don't have one city in this country that can honestly say it is an example of sincere integration.

Malcolm X: The FBI Files, page 232

Muhammad teaches us that there is a difference between separation and segregation. Segregation is that which is forced upon inferiors by superiors. Separation is done voluntarily by two equals. You notice whenever you have an all-white school; it is not referred to as a segregated school. The Negro school is the segregated school.

Malcolm X: The FBI Files, page 233

But you take all of the integrationists, all of those who are used to finance the program of the integrationist, the average so-called Negro celebrity, put them all in one pile. And as fast as you name them off, you'll find that every one of them is married either to a white woman or a white man.

Malcolm X: The Last Speeches, page 34

Today our people can see that integrated housing has not solved our problems. At best it was only a temporary solution. One in which only the wealthy, handpicked Negroes found temporary benefit.

Malcolm X: The Last Speeches, page 67

And whereas this Uncle Tom will accept your token effort, the masses of Black people in this country are no more interested in token integration than they would be if you offered them a chance to sit inside a furnace somewhere.

Malcolm X: The Last Speeches, page 31

And this type of Negro, usually he hates Black and loves white. He doesn't want to be Black, he wants to be white. And he'll get on his bended knees and beg you for integration, which means he would rather live - rather than live with his own kind who love him, he'll force himself to live in neighborhoods around white people whom he knows don't mean him any good.

Malcolm X: The Last Speeches, page 32

-Separation-

And this is the thing that white people in America have to come to realize. That there are two types of Black people in this country. One who identifies with you so much so he will let you brutalize him and still beg you for a chance to sit next to you. And then there's the one who's not interested in sitting next to you. He's not interested in being around you. He's not interested in what you have. He wants something of his own. He wants to someplace where he can call his own. He doesn't want a seat in your restaurant where you can give him some old bad coffee or bad food. He wants his own restaurant. And he wants some land where he can build that restaurant on, in a city that it can go in. He wants something of his own.

Malcolm X: The Last Speeches, page 30

The Honorable Elijah Muhammad says the only way to solve the problem of the so-called Negro is complete separation in the United States. ...The Honorable Elijah Muhammad says, every effort on the part of the government up till now to solve this problem by bringing about a just, equitable situation between whites and Blacks mixed up together here in this house has failed. Has failed absolutely. So he says since you can't give the Negro justice in your house let us leave this house and go back home.

Malcolm X: The Last Speeches, page 50

-Women-

One thing I noticed in both the Middle East and Africa, in every country that was progressive, the women were progressive. In every country that was underdeveloped and backward, it was to the same degree that the women were undeveloped, or underdeveloped, and backwards.

Malcolm X: The Last Speeches, page 18

-Education-

Education is an important element in the struggle for human rights. It is the means to help our children and our people rediscover their identity and thereby increase their self-respect. Education is our passport to the future, for tomorrow, belongs only to the people who prepare for it today.

Malcolm X: By Any Means Necessary
(OAAU Founding Rally), page 43

Our children are being criminally shortchanged in the public schools system of America.

Malcolm X: By Any Means Necessary, page 43

When we send our children to school they learn nothing about us other than that we used to be cotton pickers. Every little child going to school thinks his grandfather was a cotton picker. Why, your grandfather was Toussaint L'Overture; your grandfather was Hannibal.

Your grandfather was some of the greatest Black people who walked the earth. It was your grandfather's hands who forged civilization and it was your grandfather's hands who rocked the cradle of civilization. But the textbooks tell our children nothing about the great contributions of Afro-Americas to the growth and development of this country.

Malcolm X: By Any Means Necessary, page 43-44

... just because you have colleges and universities, doesn't mean you have education. The colleges and universities in the American educational system are skillfully used to mis-educate.

Malcolm X: By Any Means Necessary, page 160-161

-Power-

Basically there are two kinds of power that count in America: economic power and political power, with social power being derived from those two.

Malcolm X: By Any Means Necessary, page 45-46

-Religion-

.... I'm sorry to say, but it's true, many Negro preachers, religious leaders, know absolutely nothing about the origin of their own denominations, the origin and history of Christianity, and they know much less about the religions of Africa and Asia.

Malcolm X: The FBI Files, page 187

Brothers and sisters, the white man has brainwashed us black people to fasten our gaze upon a blond-haired, blue eyed Jesus! We're worshiping a Jesus that doesn't even look like us! Oh, yes! Now just bear with me, listen to the teachings of the Messenger of Allah, the Honorable Elijah Muhammad. Now just think of this. The blond-haired, blue eyed white man has taught you and me to worship a white Jesus, and shout and sing and pray to this God that's his God, the white man's God. The white man has taught us to shout and sing and pray until we die, to wait until death, while this white man has his milk and honey in the streets paved with gold dollars here on this earth.

Martin & Malcolm & America, page 151

No religion will ever make me forget the condition of our people in this country. No religion will ever make me forget the continued fighting with dogs against our people in this country. No religion will make me forget the police clubs that come up'side our heads. No God, no religion, no nothing will make me forget until it stops, until it's finished, until it's eliminated. I want to make that point clear.

Malcolm x Speaks (The Harlem Hate Gang Scare), page 10

The Christian world usually is what we call the Western world. Now what do I think, what is my image? The exploitation, colonization of the dark nations or.... lands was done by nations that today are known as Christian powers. Christians made slaves here in America out of twenty million Black people who today are called second class citizens.... The people of Africa ... today... are trying to get free from countries who represented themselves to the Africans as Christian nations.... Wherever you find dark people or non-white people today ... trying to get freedom, they are trying to get freedom from the people who represent themselves as Christians; and if you go to them and ask them their picture of a Christian, they'll tell you "an exploiter, a slave master." In America the definition would be one who promises you equal rights for a hundred years and never gives it to you.

Martin & Malcolm &America, *page 169*

Christianity is the White man's religion. The Holy Bible in the White man's hands and his interpretation of it have been the greatest single ideological weapon for enslaving millions of non-white human beings. Every country the white man has conquered with his guns, he has always paved the way, and salved his conscience, by carrying the Bible and interpreting it to call people "heathens,, and "pagans;" then he sends his guns, then his missionaries behind the guns to mop up.

Martin & Malcolm & America, *page 166*

The hardest test I ever faced in life was praying. .... Picking a lock to rob someone's house was the only way my knees had ever been bent before. I had to force myself to bend my knees. And waves of shame and embarrassment would force me back up. For evil to bend its knees, admitting its guilt, to implore the forgiveness of God, is the hardest thing in the world.

Martin & Malcolm & America, page 156

Christ wasn't white. Christ was a Black man.

Malcolm X: As They Knew Him, page 118

A man's choice of religion is his personal business.

Malcolm X: By Any Means Necessary, page 115

I believe in a religion that believes in freedom.

Malcolm X: By Any Means Necessary, page 115

-Martin Luther King and Others-

At any rate, I will challenge Roy Wilkins at anytime, anywhere and under any conditions to a public debate concerning his charges that we who follow the Muslim faith are no better or are no different than the Ku Klux Klan, especially when there are over six hundred million Muslims on this earth that stretch from the China Seas to the shores of West Africa and here in America.

Malcolm X: The FBI Files, *page 183*

They were talking about how they were going to march on Washington.... That they were going to march on Washington, march on the Senate, march on the White House, march on Congress, and tie it up, bring it to a halt, not let the government proceed. They even said they were going out to the airport and lay on the runway and not let any airplanes land. I'm telling you what they said ...That was the Black revolution.

Malcolm X: The FBI Files, *page 36*

I'll tell one of the dangers of Martin Luther King. King himself is probably a good man, means well and all that, But the danger is that white people use King. They use King to satisfy their own fears. They blow him up. They give him power beyond his actual influence. Because they want to believe within themselves that Negroes are non-violent and patient, and long suffering and forgiving. White people want to believe that so bad, cause they're so guilty. But the danger is, when they blow up King and fool themselves into thinking that Negroes are really nonviolent, and patient and long suffering; they've got a powder keg in their house.

And instead of them trying to do something to defuse the powder keg, they're putting a blanket over it, trying to make believe that this is no powder keg; that this is a couch that we can lay on and enjoy.

"Malcolm X As They Knew Him", *Page 178*

White people follow King. White People pay King. White people subsidize King. White people support King. But the masses don't support Martin Luther King. King is the best weapon that the white man, who wants brutalize Negroes, has ever gotten in this country, because he is setting up a situation where, when the white man wants to attack Negroes, they can't defend themselves, because King has put this foolish philosophy out - you're not supposed ... to defend yourself.

Martin & Malcolm & America, *page 108*

Any Negro who teaches other Negroes to turn the other cheek is disarming that Negro. Any Negro who teaches Negroes to turn the other cheek in the face of attack is disarming that Negro of his God given right, of his moral right, of his natural right, of his intelligent right to defend himself. Everything in nature can defend itself, and is right in defending itself except the American Negro. And men like [Martin Luther] King -their job is to go among the Negroes and teach Negroes, "Don't fight back." He doesn't tell them, "Don't fight each other." "Don't fight the white man" is what is what he is saying in essence, because the followers of Martin Luther King, Jr, will cut each other from head to foot, but they will not do anything to defend themselves against the attacks of the white man. But King's philosophy falls upon the ears of only a small minority. The majority or masses of black people in this country are more inclined in the direction of the Honorable Elijah Muhammad than Martin Luther King, Jr.

"Malcolm X As They Knew Him", Page 138

... And it is good for white people to know this. Because if white people get the impression that Negroes all endorse this old tum-the-other-cheek cowardly philosophy of Dr. Martin Luther King, then whites are going to make the mistake of putting their hands on some Black man, thinking he's going to turn the other cheek, and he'll end up losing his hand and losing his life in the try.

Malcolm X: The Last Speeches, *page 40*

-The News Media-

What the press fails to point out is that no Muslims go to prison. Those men weren't Muslims before they went to prison. Those men were Christians before they went to prison.

Malcolm X: The FBI Files, page 235

We had meetings where we let white reporters come in. They did nothing but distort what was said or took it out of context, or blew up what they considered to be negative. They don't come to listen objectively and then go out and report objectively; they go out to project us as a racist group, as a Black supremacist group, or as a group that is advocating violence.

Malcolm X: The FBI Files, page 236

But when you become politically independent in this country, the white media, they label you a racist. The reason for this is, the only way you can become politically independent of the white political machine is to have the support of the Black masses. The only way you can get the support of the Black masses is to say how they think and how they feel. And when you begin to speak to the Black masses, how they feel and think, then the whites call you a racist. Because you have to talk in the context of the intense degree of dissatisfaction that exists in the Negro community.

Malcolm X: The Last Speeches, *page 79*

The press whips up hysteria in the white public. Then it shifts gears and starts working trying to get the sympathy of the white public. And then it shifts gears and gets the white public to support whatever criminal action they're getting ready to involve the United States in.

Malcolm X: The Last Speeches, *page 164*

it's imagery. They [news media] use their ability to create images, and then they use these images that they've created to mislead the people. To confuse the people and make the people accept wrong as right and reject right as wrong. Make the people actually think that the criminal is the victim and the victim is the criminal.

Malcolm X: The Last Speeches, *page 165*

-Self Defense-

If you take up arms you'll end it , but if you sit around and wait for the one who's in power to make up his mind that he should end it, then you will be waiting for a long time.

Malcolm X: The FBI Files, page 310

I think that you will find a Muslim never attacks anyone, but that Muslim is within his God given rights to retaliate against anyone who attacks him. He is never to be the aggressor, but the Holy Koran teaches us to fight against those who fight against us.

Malcolm X: The FBI Files, page 239

I'm nonviolent with those who are nonviolent with me. But when you drop that violence on me, then you've made me go insane, and I'm not responsible for what I do.

Malcolm X Speaks (The Ballot or The Bullet), page 34

-Pan Africanism-

Unity between the Africans of the West and the Africans of the fatherland will well change the course of history.

Malcolm X Speaks, page 62

Africa will not go forward any faster than we will and we will not go forward any faster than Africa will. We have one destiny and we've had one past.

Malcolm X: By Any Means Necessary
(OAAU Founding Rally), page 40

It is time for the African Americans to become an integral part of the world's Pan-Africanists, and even though we might remain in America physically while fighting for the benefits the Constitution guarantees us, we must "return" to Africa philosophically and culturally and develop a working unity in the framework of Pan-Africanism.

Malcolm X Speaks", page 63

To the same degree Africa is independent and respected we are independent and respected, but to the degree we are disrespected the Africans are also disrespected. Our origin is the same and our destiny is the same, whether we like it or not.

Malcolm X: By Any Means Necessary
(At a Meeting in Paris), page 122

-Thinking for Oneself-

A man who tosses worms in the river isn't necessarily a friend of the fish. All the fish who take him for a friend, who think the worm's got no hook in it, usually end up in the frying pan.

Malcolm X: As They Knew Him, page 117-118

One of the best ways to safeguard yourself from being deceived is always to form the habit of looking at things for yourself, listening to things for yourself, thinking for yourself, before you try and come to any judgement. Never base your impression of someone on what someone else has said. Or upon what someone else has written. Or upon what you read about someone that somebody else wrote. Never base your judgement on things like that.

Especially in this kind of country and in this kind of society which has mastered the art of very deceitfully painting people whom they don't like in an image that they know you won't like.

So you end up hating your friends and loving your enemies.

Malcolm X Speaks, *page 91*

I want to point this out to you; I don't let anybody choose my friends. And you shouldn't let anybody choose your friends. You and I practice the habit of weighing people and situations and weighing groups and weighing governments for ourselves. And don't let somebody else tell us who our enemies should be and who our friends should be.

"Malcolm X Speaks", *page 102*

... And just analyze and analyze; and question things that you don't understand, so we can at least try and get a better picture of what faces us.

"Malcolm X Speaks", *page 118*

But if you form the habit of taking what someone else says about a thing without checking it out for yourself, you'll find that other people will have you hating your friends and loving your enemies. This is one of the things that our people are beginning to learn today - that it is very important to think out a situation for yourself. If you don't do it, you'll always be maneuvered into a situation where you are never fighting your actual enemies, where you will find yourself fighting your own self.

Malcolm x Speaks, page 138

And the poor so-called Negro doesn't have his own name, doesn't have his own language, doesn't have his own culture, doesn1t have his own country. He doesn't even have his own mind. And he thinks that he's Black 'cause God cursed him. He's not Black because God cursed him. He's Black because - rather he's cursed because he's out of his mind. He has lost his mind. He has a white mind instead of the type of mind he should have.

Malcolm X: The Last Speeches, page 33

-Black/African American Unity-

Our people have made the mistake of confusing the methods with the objectives. As long as we agree on the objectives, we should never fall out with each other just because we believe in different methods or tactics or strategy to reach a common objective.

Malcolm X Speaks (The Black Revolution), page 51

In my recent travels into the African countries and the others, it was impressed upon me the importance of having a working unity among all peoples, black as well as white. But the only way this is going to be brought about is that the black ones have to be in unity first.

Malcolm X Speaks (The Harlem Hate Gang Scare), page 70

In the future we will emphasize unity of the Black man for economic, financial and moral betterment.

Malcolm X: The FBI Files

I think all of us should be critics of each other. Whenever you can't stand criticism you can never grow. I don't think that it serves any purpose for the leaders of our people to waste their time fighting each other needlessly. I think that we accomplish more when we sit down in private and iron out whatever differences that may exist and try and then do something constructive for the benefit of our people.

Malcolm X: The Last Speeches, page 87

-Forming Coalitions with Non Black Progressive Groups/People-

We will work with anyone, with any group, no matter what their color is as long as they are genuinely interested in taking the type of steps necessary to bring an end to the injustices that black people in this country are afflicted by. No matter what their color is, no matter what their political, economic or social philosophy is, as long as their aims and objectives are in the direction of destroying the vulturous system that has been sucking the blood of black people in this country. They're alright with us. But if they're in anyway that compromising, dangerous type of person, then we think they should be dealt with.

Malcolm X Speaks The Harlem Hate Gang Scare, page 70-71

-Revolution and Revolutionary Movements-

Revolutions are fought to get control of land, to remove the absentee landlord and gain control of that land and the institutions that flow from that land.

Malcolm X Speaks (The Black Revolution), page 57

This is all we want -to be human a being. If we can't be recognized and respected as a human being, we have to create a situation where no human being will enjoy life, liberty, and the pursuit of happiness.

__Malcolm X: By Any Means Necessary,__ page 86

-Self Hate-

He calls himself an American Negro - a Negro in America. And usually he'll deny his own race, his own color, just to be a second class American. He'll deny his history, his own culture. He'll deny all his brothers and sisters in Africa, in Asia, in the East, just to be a second class American. He denies everything that he represents or everything that was in his past, just to be accepted into a country and into a government that has rejected him ever since he was brought here.

__Malcolm X: The Last Speeches,__ page 34

Our color became to us a chain. - we felt that it was holding us back; our color became to us like a prison which we felt was keeping us confined, not letting us go this way or that way. We felt that all of these restrictions were based solely upon our color, and the psychological reaction to that would have to be that as long as we felt imprisoned or chained or trapped by Black skin, Black features, and Black blood, that skin and those features and that blood holding us back automatically had to become hateful to us. It made us feel inferior; it made us feel inadequate; made us helpless. And when we fell victims of this feeling of inadequacy or inferiority or helplessness, we turned to somebody to show us the way.

Martin & Malcolm & America, page 291

When I pointed out that there are two kinds of Negroes - some Negroes don't want a Black man to speak for them. That type of Negro doesn't even want to be Black. He's ashamed of being Black. And you'll never hear him refer to himself as Black. Now that type we don't pretend to speak for you. You can speak for him. In fact you can have him.

Malcolm X: The Last Speeches, page 28

So you have two types of Negro. The old type and the new type. Most of you know the old type. When you read about him in history during slavery he was called "Uncle Tom." He was the house Negro. And during slavery you had two Negroes. You had the house Negro and the field Negro. The house Negro usually lived close to his master. He dressed like his master. He wore his master's second hand clothes. He ate food that his master left on the table. And he lived in his master's house - probably in the basement or the attic - but he still lived in the master's house. So whenever that house Negro identified himself, he always identified himself in the same sense that his master identified himself. When his master said, "We have good food," the house Negro would say, "Yes; we have plenty of good food." When the master said that "we have a fine home here," the house Negro said "Yes, we have a fine home here." When the master would be sick, the house Negro identified so much with his master he'd say, "What's the matter boss, we sick?" His master's pain was his pain. And it hurt him more for his master to be sick than for him to be sick himself. When the house started burning down, that type of Negro would fight harder to put the master's house out than the master himself would. But then you had another Negro out in the field. The house Negro was in the minority. The masses the field Negroes were the masses. They were in the majority. When the master got sick, they prayed that he'd die. If his house caught on fire, they'd pray for a wind to come and fan the breeze. If someone came to the House Negro and said, "Let's go, let's separate," naturally that Uncle Tom would say, "Go where? What could I do without boss? Where would I live? How would I dress? Who would look out for me?" That's the house Negro. But if you went to the field Negro and said, "Let's separate," he wouldn't even ask you where or how. He'd say, 'Yes, let's go." And that one ended right there.

Malcolm X: The Last Speeches, pages 28-29

You have taken a man who is Black on the outside and made him white on the inside. His brain is white as snow. His heart is white as snow. And therefore, whenever you say, this is ours, he thinks he's white the same as you, so what's yours he thinks is his. Even right down to your woman.

Malcolm X: The Last Speeches, page 31

And the poor so-called Negro doesn't have his own name, doesn't have his language, doesn't have his own culture, doesn't have his own history. He doesn't have his own country. He doesn't even have his own mind. And he thinks that he's Black 'cause God cursed him. He's not Black 'cause God cursed him. He's Black because -rather he's cursed because he's out of his mind. He has lost his mind. He has a white mind instead of the type of mind that he should have.

Malcolm X: The Last Speeches, page 33

When you teach a man to hate his lips that God gave him, the shape of his nose that God gave him, the texture of his hair that God gave him, the color of the skin that God gave him, you've committed the worst crime that a race of people can commit.

Malcolm X: The Last Speeches, page 166-167

-Interracial Marriages-

Subconsciously a Negro doesn't have any respect or regard or confidence, nor can he be moved by, another Black man who marries a white woman or a Black woman who marries a white man.

Malcolm X: The Last Speeches, page 34

When you are dealing with humanity as one family, there's no question of integration or intermarriage. It's just one human being marrying another human being, or one human being living around and with another human being.

Malcolm X: As They Knew Him, page 187

-Being an African American-

I believe that when you are a Black man born in this particular society, you are faced with certain dangers already.

Malcolm X: The FBI Files, page 347

-Retribution-

The book says that the sins of the fathers will be visited upon the heads of the children even unto the seventh generation.

Malcolm X: The Last Speeches, page 77

.... I don't think that any power can enslave a people and not look forward to having that injustice come back upon itself.

Malcolm X: The Last Speeches, page 107

-Being Sent to Prison-

I was finally caught and spent seventy-seven months in three different prisons. But it was the greatest thing that ever happened to me, because it was in prison that I first heard the teachings of the Honorable Elijah Muhammad. His teachings were what turned me around.

Malcolm X: As They Knew Him, page 124

I often think sir, that in 1946, I was sentenced to eight to ten years in Cambridge, Massachusetts, as a common thief who had never passed the eighth grade. And the next time I went back to Cambridge was in March 1961, as a guest speaker at the Harvard Law School Forum.

Malcolm X: As They Knew Him, page 124

-Criticism-

Whenever you can't stand criticism you can never grow.

Malcolm X: The Last Speeches, page 87

Figure 1

Malcom Little's Mugshot: proof that God can both change and use anyone for His Divine Purpose

Figure 2

Malcolm X with the "Louisville Lip" Cassius Clay / Muhammad Ali

Figure 3

Malcolm X in a Reflective Mood

Figure 4

Malcolm X in three obvious poses of deep thought

Figure 5

Malcolm X speaks about the "Pedagogy of the Oppressed"

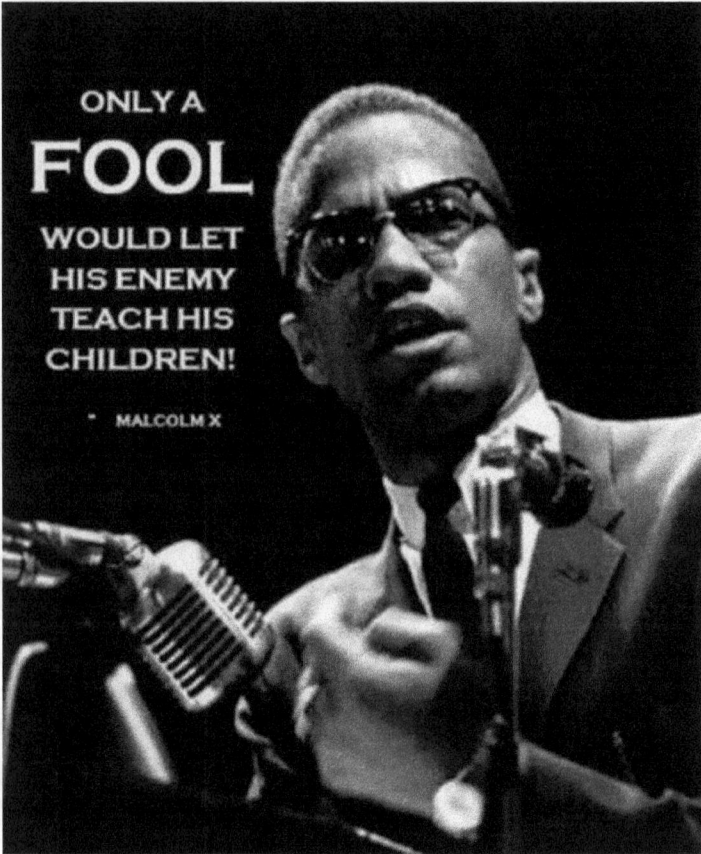

ONLY A
FOOL
WOULD LET
HIS ENEMY
TEACH HIS
CHILDREN!

- MALCOLM X

Figure 6

Malcolm X with Dr. Martin Luther King

Figure 7

Malcolm X addresses the issue of standing on principles

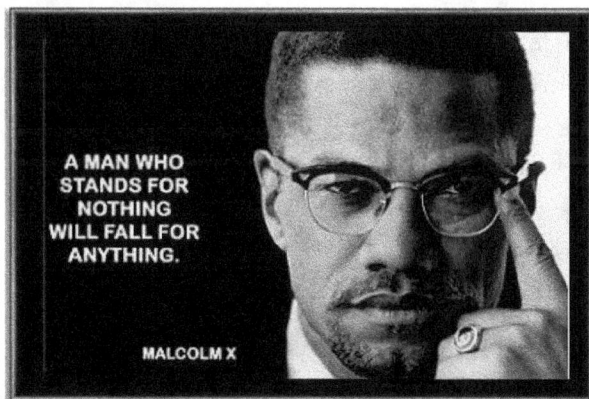

Figure 8

Malcolm X standing ready to defend his family and beliefs by "Any Means Necessary"

Figure 9

Malcolm X possibly contemplating his next speech or action

Figure 10

Malcolm X addresses the issue of education

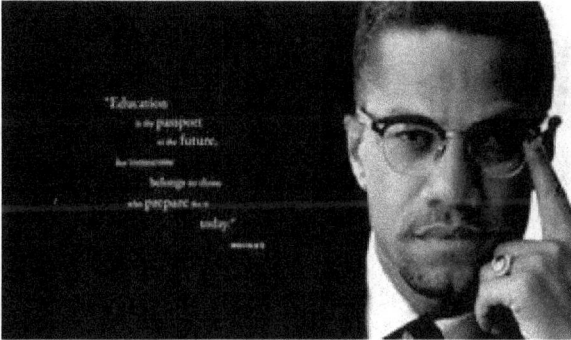

Figure 11

Malcolm X in a defiant posture

Figure 12

Malcolm X speaks on being prepared for the future

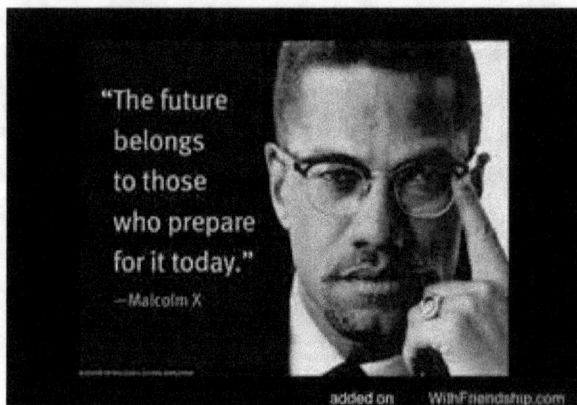

Figure 13

Malcolm X in a very relaxed posture

Figure 14

Malcolm X the devoted family man – husband and father

Figure 15

Malcolm X speaks on sincerity

I want to be remembered as someone that was sincere even if I made mistakes, they were in sincerity. If I was wrong, I was wrong in sincerity. I can deal with a person that's wrong, as long as they are sincere.

Malcolm X

Figure 16

Malcolm X in a contemplative mood

Figure 17

Malcolm X speaks on the influence of the media

Figure 18

Malcolm X on avoiding religious differences

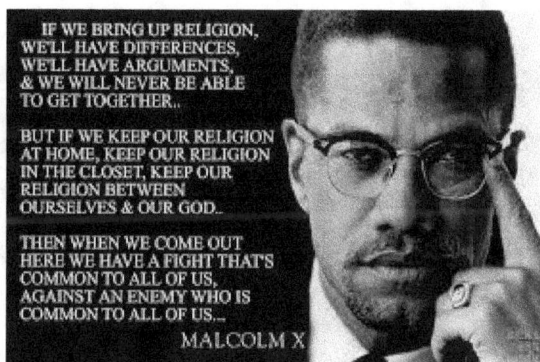

IF WE BRING UP RELIGION,
WE'LL HAVE DIFFERENCES,
WE'LL HAVE ARGUMENTS,
& WE WILL NEVER BE ABLE
TO GET TOGETHER...

BUT IF WE KEEP OUR RELIGION
AT HOME, KEEP OUR RELIGION
IN THE CLOSET, KEEP OUR
RELIGION BETWEEN
OURSELVES & OUR GOD...

THEN WHEN WE COME OUT
HERE WE HAVE A FIGHT THAT'S
COMMON TO ALL OF US,
AGAINST AN ENEMY WHO IS
COMMON TO ALL OF US...

MALCOLM X

Figure 19

Malcolm X speaks on adversity

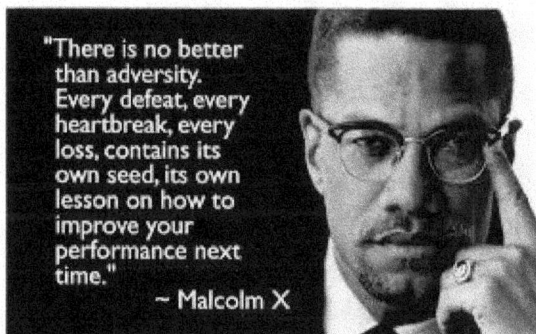

"There is no better
than adversity.
Every defeat, every
heartbreak, every
loss, contains its
own seed, its own
lesson on how to
improve your
performance next
time."
~ Malcolm X

Figure 20

Malcolm X speaks on condemning others

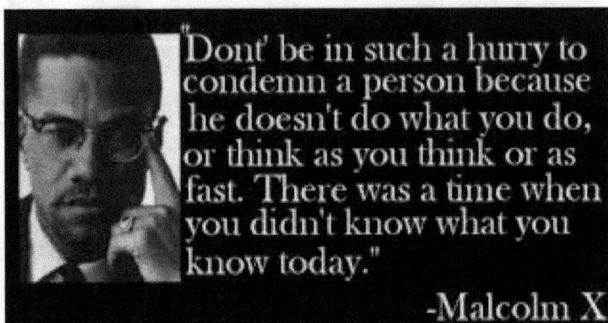

"Dont' be in such a hurry to condemn a person because he doesn't do what you do, or think as you think or as fast. There was a time when you didn't know what you know today."

-Malcolm X

Bibliography

Breitman, George. Malcolm X: The Man and His Ideas. New York: Grove Press, 1965

Breitman, George. Malcolm X Speaks. New York: Grove Press, 1966

Breitman, George. Malcolm X: By Any Means Necessary. New York: Pathfinder Press, 1970

Carson, Clayborne. Malcolm X: The FBI File. New York: Carroll & Graf Publishers, Inc. 1991

Clarke, John Henrik. Malcolm X: The Man and His Times. Trenton, New Jersey: Africa World Press, 1990

Cone, James, H. Martin & Malcolm & America: A Dream Or A Nightmare. Maryknoll, New York: Orbis Books, 1992

Gallen, David. Malcolm X As They Knew Him. New York: Carroll & Graf Publishers, Inc. 1992

Perry, Bruce. Malcolm X: The Last Speeches. New York. Pathfinder Press, 1989

X, Malcolm. The Autobiography of Malcolm X. New York: Grove Press Inc. 1964

X, Malcolm. Malcolm X On Afro-American History. New York: Pathfinder Press Inc. 1967 Malcolm X: The End of White Supremacy: Four Speeches New York: Merlin House Inc., 1971

CREDITS

Book Cover Concept   Brother James

Book Cover Art Work   Tim James

Book Cover Synthesis   Steven L. Hill

Original Book Cover Art Work   Brother James

Figures 1-20 were taken from photographs on the public Domain of the WWW/Internet using the Images feature of Google.

www.ingramcontent.com/pod-product-compliance
Lightning Source LLC
Chambersburg PA
CBHW050552280326
41933CB00011B/1808